Dedicated to those cast away.

The Wet Hex

Also by Sun Yung Shin

Rough, and Savage
Skirt Full of Black
Unbearable Splendor

The
Wet Hex

SUN YUNG SHIN

COFFEE HOUSE PRESS
Minneapolis
2022

Coffee House Press books are available to the trade through our pri-
mary distributor, Consortium Book Sales & Distribution, cbsd.com or
(800) 283-3572. For personal orders, catalogs, or other information,
write to info@coffeehousepress.org.

Coffee House Press is a nonprofit literary publishing house. Support
from private foundations, corporate giving programs, government
programs, and generous individuals helps make the publication of
our books possible. We gratefully acknowledge their support in detail
in the back of this book.

LIBRARY OF CONGRESS CATALOGING-IN-PUBLICATION DATA
Names: Shin, Sun Yung, author.
Title: The wet hex / Sun Yung Shin.
Description: Minneapolis : Coffee House Press, 2022.
Identifiers: LCCN 2021059295 (print) | LCCN 2021059296 (ebook) |
    ISBN 9781566896382 (paperback) | ISBN 9781566896467 (epub)
Subjects: LCGFT: Poetry.
Classification: LCC PS3619.H575 W48 2022 (print) |
    LCC PS3619.H575 (ebook) | DDC 811/.6—dc23/eng/20211217
LC record available at https://lccn.loc.gov/2021059295
LC ebook record available at https://lccn.loc.gov/2021059296

PRINTED IN THE UNITED STATES OF AMERICA
31 30 29 28 27 26 25 24   2 3 4 5 6 7 8 9

... Praise our

mothers of lost habitats, mothers of fallout, mothers
of extinction—*pray for us*—because even tomorrow
will be haunted—*leave them, leave us, leave*—

—Craig Santos Perez, from "Halloween
in the Anthropocene, 2015"

"And the priest shall write these curses in a book, and he shall
blot *them* out with the bitter water: And he shall cause the woman
to drink the bitter water that causeth the curse: and the water that
causeth the curse shall enter into her, *and become* bitter."

—Numbers 5:23, Holy Bible, King James Version

"Hex" meaning "magic spell" was first recorded in 1909.
Earlier it meant "witch," see "hag," meaning "repulsive old woman"
probably from Old English: *hægtes, hægtesse* "witch, sorceress,
enchantress, fury." It is a word that has no male cognate.

CONTENTS

The Wet Hex

Translate This Body into Everything

with thanks to Harryette Mullen

Here I am at the inconvenience
store of unspoken words. Rows of soft
silence. The produce
of our Korean families. Five thousand years

+

of the People in White. We are the girls
who went away, who left memory behind,
who ate pebbles and stopped talking.
We each need a librarian, an army of

+

alphabets to keep us warm at night,
when our voices stiffen to copper and tin.
When our grandmothers dissolve into mist
and our grandfathers mold wives out of dirt.

+

Here we are at the corner of the past and fate
no one discovered except American day
by American night. Work. Switching faces was easier
than trading one tongue for another.

+

How do we pronounce our skin in English,
turn our silences inside out like a fox-fur stole.
The Korean fox with nine tails is a demon,
always a woman, her heart thick with dreams

+

of human sacrifice, of the future of nature.
Korean girls who slept with the dictionary
so they would never be alone, so one day
they could give birth to bruises and poetry.

(Section 1)

THERE IS / NEVER / ENOUGH

A Spade Is for Piercing the Ground and a Shovel Is for Heaving

Preparations begin now, in the middle of my life—
death was born with me, didn't expect to change languages,
might not know when it is called. Sometimes English sits on the
   surface of the skin.

We are water, we are rivers of descent;
gravity is inevitable yet grievable.
Mourn as you like, death is another migration.

Bring the body home and gently lay it down on its back,
bind tightly the hands and feet of the corpse,
do this to keep it from running away like a lonely child—

carry the coat it wore (when it was a person) to the roof—
a flag of surrender, a signal flag to the spirit world, *new arrival*;
call out the name of the dead three times.

Perfume the bath water—the death of a thousand flowers—
comb the hair and catch what falls,
what was grown from the body must accompany the body.

Manicure the fingernails and toenails,
carefully reserve the nail trimmings,
the hair and nails are to be collected into five pouches for the coffin.

Obtain a spoon made from a willow tree, it is a lightweight hardwood,
not heavy in the mouth—
feed the corpse three spoonfuls of uncooked rice: *one thousand, two
   thousand, three thousand bushels.*

Slide metal coins into the mouth—the spirit journey can be costly, the
   way long—
cloak the body in the death dress of hemp or silk,

envelop the body with a quilted cloth, and bind the body with ropes
    seven times.

Transport the body on a decorated bier out of the house—for this you
    need the living—
observe it float heavily toward the gate. Not unlike a boat
the bier is decorated with fierce dragons and phoenixes; colorful dolls
    guard the dead.

On the way out of the household premises, lower the bier three times—
the dead's final departure from home is marked with this ritual
    bowing.
At the grave, the shaman will exorcise evil spirits from the site. Pay
    the shaman.

Submerge the coffin in the open ground, it has already been emptied,
    given its duty,
yes, like another mouth, or a box for a smaller box—one by one,
the ground is a wound that heals, that embraces its lost materials.

Mines and Museums, or, the DMZ Is a Nature Preserve

The wreck of human invention tastes of space
Most borders are invitation of affliction
Most borders make orphans
Mines wind down under a layer of earth like clocks and roots

The ghosts of burned trees dream in Russian
While in the multiverse the mannequins abandon their cosmonaut
     suits in the museums
What are these trenches but future (museums)

In the weaponry of space; all the earth is a mine
Compactor and gardener of deaths yet to burgeon

Our eyes at the front of our heads to fox and fix
Prey on the horizon; moving as if on a track
Sightlines rings of planetary wax museums; dark matter
In space there are no seasons

*

Saturn is Rome's god of agriculture; god of time god of dissolution
Treasury and revelry
The god-milk of temporal adjustments
The gods of role reversals; nurseries and the orphan's premonitions
A curse requires no special rituals

Another name *Sterculius* from *stercus* meaning dung meaning life
     from death
Meaning shit and sun and seeds
And baptism of your godchild and the drowning the river

The difference between a museum and a tomb
A bomb is not a metaphor
I wore a belt made of ice; I grew with child, a child of ice
and all along—my mother: a glacier, a shipwreck

Behind This Door Is a Siberian Tiger

A child born in the Year of the Tiger
is destined to split apples, collect matchbooks, and speak
the language of fire-in-the-field.
A poet can make the sun jealous.

To use magic to become small, to stow away
in hollow logs, to polish her claws so smooth
they reflect last month's moonlight.

Let us talk about light. How does your mother
pronounce it. How does your father bury it.
How does your brother borrow against it,
betting everything God promised.

A child born in any Year of the Tiger
hoards this inheritance. Wears careless stripes
even to bed. This is her wealth.

A tiger is a poet, she lives in the wanton rustle of grass.
The wind spills words at the foot of the tree,
whisks a path beyond here, past whole cities of tigers,
past easy recognition, into communion.

An Orphan Receives Her Commercial DNA Test Results from Two Companies: An Abecedarian

Ancestry laid upon a curse, a jinx

Blood, and another thing molten—reveries of my face, the façade
    behind my face

Called to account the countries, deviations of echolocations:

Dead—mine—dark-detained

Ever banked in an ethnographic afterlife.

Fell—deep sleep postponing my rewrite, rotate, mutate;

Genes to be circumnavigated by spit-polished explorers.

How is a child's globe a work of colonial conditioning?

In this condition, the wet hex in miniature

Jumps from gene sequence to succession. Pattern recognition:

Kinship, failing upriver—descent—

Life maps itself in vials sent via the real

Mail, archaic method homesick for the gold horses of its origins.

Never miscalculate genealogical disruption's (in)ability;

Orphan your ancestors in the underworld; above—who tends graves,

Pours the prayer of soju when the dead need music. Shall this be our final

Quarry, silent as a doe and daughter,

Reading the light, sewing a shade; a haunting

Sold to a centrifuge, the sterile shine of its exposed aperture—now

Travel to the Neander Tal; witness the heavy-brow-boned branch fork
    and break. Our dead

Underestimate us, time machines drifting at the rate of future's arrival,

Venn diagrams of past and speculation

Where will we repose. Collected. Finger- and jawbone; dusted dictionary

Xenomorph, alien self, foreign

You, incarnate in the disciplined nation of the contemporaneous;
    stranger

Zealous for the sweet peace of the unborn, as yet unburied.

Castaways in Paradise

"'What brings you here,' he asked. 'What do you seek in this high tower, Phaëthon—you, an heir no parent would deny?'

'They saw tracks of animals— goats, the men assumed, but actually deer—but found the corpse of only one. Like so much else in the other word, they knew not what to make of the sight.

The father put aside his shining crown and told him to draw nearer and took him in his arms: 'It would not be appropriate for me to disavow our relationship.'

Consumed by the idea of this small child alone in the wilderness, Columbus intervened, pledging the boy 'to God and fortune.'

How often she would be too terrified to lie down by herself in the deep woods, and wandered to the fields near her old home/. . . Often she hid herself at the sight of beasts, forgetting that she was a beast herself. And the bear was frightened by the sight of bears up in the mountains—and afraid of wolves, although her father had been changed to one.

Columbus assumed that the object 'must be those of some ancestors of the family; because those houses were of a kind where many persons live in one, and they should be relations descended from only one.'

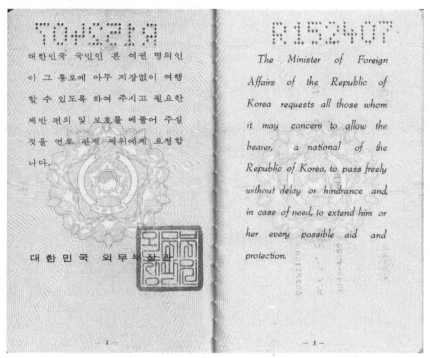

대한민국 국민인 본 여권 명의인 이 그 통로에 아무 지장없이 여행 할 수 있도록 하여 주시고 필요한 제반 편의 및 보호를 베풀어 주실 것을 연로 관계 제위에게 요청합 니다.

대 한 민 국   외 무 부 장 관

The Minister of Foreign Affairs of the Republic of Korea requests all those whom it may concern to allow the bearer, a national of the Republic of Korea, to pass freely without delay or hindrance and, in case of need, to extend him or her every possible aid and protection.

'To keep her from successfully appealing to Jupiter, her speech was snatched away: only a growl from deep within her chest, a rumble, hoarse and menacing, remained.'

A pile of bare human bones testified to their predilection: 'All that could be gnawed on, had been gnawed on, and all that was left, was what could not be eaten, because it was inedible.'"

History of Domestication

Child. Put your name in a hat, or a volcano.
      Your sense of time is inadequate.

Maiden. While I sleep my secret face faces the other way.
      Grief is a heated iron comb.

Wife. The kerosene of grief. It doesn't age well. It degrades.
      Grief is a kind of time.

Mother. Sign your name. Become a series of signals.
      Holes punched through a rag. Make a space to look through.
      Your eye is a hole, too.
      Your iris constricts a telegraphy of the future.

Elder. Strange deliveries.
      The midwifery of anything here.
      Trade this hide for sod.

Yesterday. At night I dream of an infant made of flour and heat.
      We dream of the castaway wind inside us.

Today. At night my throat dresses itself in jewel-green feathers.
      It does. You do.

How an Animal Knows Where She Ends
   and You Begin

I heard your mother asked you, *Where are the edges of your body*
                                        You replied, *Jump rope is a cable of howl*

We read that the rope is not a lead but a whip
                              You saw that a crop scoops the air out of space
Space flogs the air and styles it a beggar
                        How the parabola arcs into geometry around the body

When the arithmetic is a kindness and not a rectangle to be buried in
            When the rope is a dragon or a divining rod
                        Translucent tables below us and the yellow
                        diamond snakes beneath

                                        A world on its cable swinging
Find in our minds the mushrooms, how they grow clandestine reveries

                        My dream fills your body like smoke
                        We have stored the lungs of the extinct in blue jars
                                    hung them like Chinese lanterns

                        Rupture into spores and lash the world to the
                        evolution of decay

Your jump line to moor everything to the beginning
                    The mares of the moon and more to fall into

                        See the row of old pins haunting the machines
                        Hold our noise fast to every threshold

An Orphan Considers the Hand of God

Mistaken for an iron spear, a copper shield,
the hands make a △, symbol of a great house,
or an ark low in the water,
or a risen fire, smoke in the distance.

How did God make his hands small enough to form the faces of so
   many soldiers?
How did he concoct my family—from rope or broth?
A child can be renamed a thousand times, or denied the dignity
   altogether.
Die without one, live without one.

A nightmare—the palest of milk-white horses;
the mother of all horses pays me a visit.
She offers me a blacksmith, to be or to marry.
Tongs, rings, hammer, anvil, forge.

She promises me my true name. Knows my ancestors, speaks their
   tongue.
Do not trust the centaur, half man, half beast.
He is cunning, as he has to be, a cursed creature.
Pretending to be the last of his kind for pity and poor lodging.

Always, the blinding bright hand of God says *No.*
God says, *I belong everywhere,*
you belong nowhere. Countries are made for the named.
Look at your identification papers. Look.

Fires burn, feed on the names of the renamed.
The golden threads of our ancestors make a ball of snakes.
Births of thousands in lightless hungry places.
Where names are expensive, where gods are for the rich.

Night is my mother. She wears many faces, has seen the glittering
    hand of God.
She pulls silver from the sky, names from the sea like fish.
There is enough. There is enough.
There is never enough.

(Section 2)

VIOLENCE IS NOT
A METAPHOR

Botany of Death

Sister, I have written your funeral in flowers/I am the last
floriographer/No more deaths after yours after mine/

I have vowed to kill death and take him with me/He shall take many
forms as my jester my wigmaker my piano player my fast horse/

Time-lapse flower film a roll of celluloid from the garden of our
school-time/Twentieth century we were caught in the fences like
rabbits/

Who were we children to sew death in our pockets like jewelry/Who
were we to save ink and hide it for epistolary exercises/

From flowers we pressed the oil and drank the wet petals/Thin velvet
tongues secret bite marks the dialectic of the slow swarm/

The hives of wasps hung like lanterns from the eaves of old trees heavy
slow silver/The smallest child unfolds the papery combs the larvae the
droplets the scent of wildflower/

Sister, die before me so I may sew words and stems all through your
body the sieve the sleeve/A body a crypt my body cryptology/Chambers
of a lock the closures on a casket/

Last change of the wound dressing last perfume death heals the ache
of life/Death seals the windows and you step through the floor the
river the last staircase/

O twin wearing a crown of stars the zodiac your fine chronometer/
There I knit and knot roots and nets/

A sky sailor a night gardener buds/barter for brightness for the food/
for the food of heat

Detonations

If pain makes the body turn to cold flame / If scars are the
photonegatives of suitable decisions / I wrote letter after letter to
the bomb maker /

I attended the bomb makers' annual ball / Shawls of white grass and
waste and fury / The earth spits its teeth at us / Giant mechanical
hummingbirds fight over all the sugar /

The Koreans scab the Japanese in the sweet cane fields / Modernity
is a rust factory / The hard soft binary / Exoskeletons make war even
harder make our bodies insects and we are home / Lay down your
lances /

All you horses sleep next to your wildness you are the shadow / Ghosts
cocktails moonlight foxfire to read by / everywhere not libraries of
the body /

War the night show the day show the violins / the rubble the child
burials the blood / Hearts the red stop signs / the graves in the air /
your black or blackened hair

Bayonets and Bonfire

Of all the things that could be fixed to the end of a rifle / For example, the face of your enemy / As a child / A prayer / Tomorrow /

The fantastic shapes of death and all the plunges over into through / After I weigh each mask and polish and oil / The better to see the mass grave in front of us / I would like to touch every face / None exactly the same not exactly /

I gave blood today / Exactly the same as yesterday / Death rejected me another day his train car full of astonished faces / The road to hell an archipelago of the dumbfounded and bewildered /

Arms the man the man the arms / A bayonet can also refer to a man armed with a bayonet /

Birds on the road birds to pluck your eye like a ripe cherry / The stone of me the pit of you fruit dreams within me fossils in the cutaways /

The siege the soldier the stab the gallop the priest and his magic oil

Specimens of Immortality

Baroque elaborations and tableaux of the Dodo / White mourning doves suspended by invisible wire /

All the rabbits wear turtle-shell helmets and face the sunrise as an army of sweet / Sentinels everywhere hidden bones like flutes of wire /

Perpetual alert to the guards of the necropolis / You are the largest of the lionesses with an assortment of cubs that died before you were born / The birth of death / Seedless grapes sewn in the vineyard /

Museum guard cultivars of boredom the gore the charge the wall of horns / Eyes everlast the horizon prey or predator / Freeze us in the hunt in the rut in the reliefless past /

My beauty is made mostly of proteins / Astringent portraiture salts and cures and trophy / Trophy with concealed bullet wounds / The soft solace of killing / The school of beauty saved from the burning /

Sightless zoo breathless savannah glass forest / Dioramas of longing / Big game hunter the new world the safari /

The feral the wild the stampede the old the lame the wounded / The wolf and the lamb lie together at the end of the world /

My horns ground to medicine / My blood blown into glass

I Wandered into a Mass Extinction Event

before I knew what was happening. I renounced my humanity (in an attempt to escape the fate of my betters and strangers).

The floods gathered up the last of the patients in small cork boats that fell from the sky (like leaves from a maple tree in autumn's last exhalation).

What was everything I could sacrifice for a Soyuz space suit? (Something worn-in and vacuum-tested.)

Just give me a sign, I said (cursing the gods and demons of my forefathers).

With the helmet's face shield down I had difficulty panning gold from the rivers of Colorado (but I said, I will prevail).

The bracelets and anklets I made with the metal *chinkled* and *chankled* (and I, caparisoned like a fine knight's horse) encouraged my prancing and unyielding vanity.

I wrote obituary after homage after ode after elegy (for every species larger than my thumb).

The flora and fauna (c)are nothing for the world of letters.

The trees recoiled (at the cannibalism of paper).

I buried every book deep, so deep a place (a place without the language of signs).

He Said That We Should Turn Back

before it was too late, before my child was born + I said, it is not a child,
it is a series of veils, each made from the silk of the worms I ate as
penance for my crimes +

What crimes, he said, *have you committed* + *None,* I said, *I was given
them as gifts,* to become the mother of all criminals +

To give birth to nothing but endless doors made of infinite texture,
texts + Pure feeling +

At the word "doors" the worms came to life and began producing skein
after reel, pure white ink + *Écriture* + White creature +

He began to slap me, punch me, kick me, and I fell to the loosened
ground, chunks of salt falling from my rough hair +

Children came startling out of the bushes to collect the salary +

Already savoring the rampion + A congregation of hungers +

Coiled on the ground, guarding my blue face, my vacant ears, all the
murk settled between them, I began to sing a lullaby +

Sleep, little thing, shutter thine eyes, bright and divine +

All the world's lakes of fire began + to plunge further into the earth

(Section 3)

THE UNDERWORLD
HOLDS ALL TETHERS

"Women in Korean myths disappear after giving birth. The reason they were born is to produce sons. But there is one myth where no female disappears. It is a fable of the foremother of shamans. Baridegi was the seventh daughter of a king and was abandoned because she was a girl. After she came back from a pilgrimage to the world of the dead, she saved her father and became the foremother of exorcists who help lead those who have died into heaven."

—김혜순 Kim Hyesoon

Gaze _ Observatory _ Threshold:
A 바리데기 Baridegi Reimagining

A sequential collaboration between Sun Yung Shin (poems)
and Jinny Yu (drawings)

I.

The king, a man under a gold hole, gave birth to a seventh daughter.

The queen, under a second, smaller gold hole, turned herself inside out, but no son could be found among the folds of her royal robes.

The king took birth.

Every child born is followed by a shadow child, their placenta.

The queen delivered the placenta, and it jumped up and landed on the windowsill and flew away, leaving a necklace of blood drops on the ground below it until it was out of sight.

The king looked at his seventh daughter and the four corners of the room turned black and empty and rose up and gathered around his head and engulfed him in darkness, as if he were an object in a 보자기 bojagi. A thick, tight, invisible knot formed over him.

He clapped his hands.

The queen caught the air between her teeth.

The king called for a box, six small doors attached at the edges, a small movable grave.

A servant brought a jade box and carved "바리데기" on the cover. *Abandoned Child.*

The newborn was placed inside the box and the box was carried to a stream and the stream decided to become thicker than jade and thus the jade box floated along with the current.

The stream made a rough, green ribbon, a long door.

A few drops of dark liquid fell onto the river as something flew by, overhead.

The water swallowed the memory and it sank to the bottom among the stones.

II.

The box called out to an old married couple passing by, *Castaway!*

The wife and husband bent over the stream and saw the jade box held by the layers of water.

(Have *you* seen water form a staircase?)

(Did you emerge from your mother by way of water, knife, or an invisible rope of shame?)

The old woman lifted the heavy lid and beheld a small pearl.

The old man looked and saw a square of fine white silk.

Not until the child gave a hearty cry did they see that it was not a pearl, and it was not a square of silk, but a baby girl.

Baridegi.

Bari gongju. Princess Abandoned.

Concentric circles. Salt, sand, glass, bone, blood.

Only one person at a time can pass gracefully through a truly round door, no matter how big it is.

When a square is placed within a circle, there is a surplus of unusable darkness.

III.

Years passed like a door glancing down at its own shadow, waxing and waning; opening, closing.

Our skeleton inside us like a second person. The marrow thinking its rich red thoughts.

The vertebral column, stacked like wood.

A fire cannot appear without its lover, air.

A princess does not exist without a king or queen first.

A king does not need a princess. Until.

The child grew to be kind, hardworking, and observant. As she rinsed the rice for the day's meals and the water grew cloudy and milky, she felt something clarifying in her spirit, as if starch were being washed away, gently.

Meanwhile, in the royal court, her father, the king, fell ill. Every medicine was brought to him.

Bark, seed, root, horn, organ, petal, oil, tea, tincture.

Spell, prayer, salt.

IV.

At the beginning of year fifteen, the king grew weaker and weaker.

The queen said, *I can almost see through you. You are becoming transparent in certain light; for example, the late afternoon.*

Perhaps your spine is made of hammered gold.

The king said, *I'm turning into air, into absence.*

Later that evening, the king fell into a deep sleep.

His bed became a vast doorway, its rich canopy became the eye of night.

It blinked its fringed lashes.

The king fell through the dark rectangle and kept falling.

V.

The king slept. A dream entered him, like smoke.

The smoke formed into a parade of small things: an iridescent fish scale, a mottled gray pebble, a white scrap of cloud.

The jury of things surrounded the king, outlining his body, and began emitting a soft hum.

He understood in his mind what they were telling him, that he was suffering, and dying, because of the seventh daughter he put into a jade box and pushed away like a regret.

If you would be well, your daughter must make a journey to the underworld. There she must obtain holy water and bring it back to you.

But are you ready to be well?

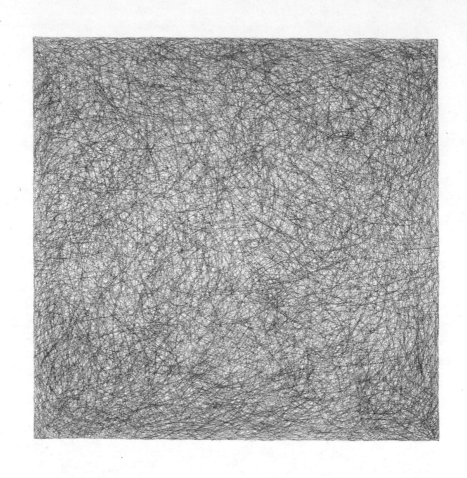

VI.

Still asleep, he received a vision of her, the princess, with her arms raised, red ropes tied along each arm, making lines to the earth.

For two more days he slumbered.

A maple tree grew up through the floor and around his platform bed.

Black vines followed, like one hundred obedient children.

On the third day, the beautiful front gates opened and the king's officials walked a girl into the compound.

The current of air from the movement of the gates reached the king, and he opened his eyes.

VII.

The girl was indeed the Princess Baridegi.

She removed her simple shoes before entering the palace.

Her shoes rested together, two small boats. It seemed as though they shared one shadow.

The queen ran to embrace her youngest daughter but first held up her girl's arms, looking for red ropes, but there were none that she could see or feel.

Baridegi bowed deeply to her parents.

The body of a child is both a debt and a time machine.

VIII.

The king told his daughter about his dream and the cure that only she could procure.

Princess Baridegi glanced down at her palms and saw *pity* and *duty*.

Her knuckles spelled *haunt* and *mercy*.

She told the parents who had abandoned her that she would save her father.

She reunited with her white shoes.

She walked back through the compound's gates and onward, beginning a journey beyond the world of the living.

The moon rose and bloomed like a flower.

IX.

One foot in front of the other, stepping on pine needles, pressing them into the brown dirt, they lay like small, headless arrows behind her.

As she got farther away, the needles began to slowly turn, orienting toward her retreating figure, like metal shavings near a magnet.

What the trees continue to gift us.

Their oil, their resin, their feathers.

Pins and needles.

A pair of hands carved from deadfall.

A princess without servants needs these shadow limbs to carry out her duty.

The cracked arms of trees above, the quilted clouds.

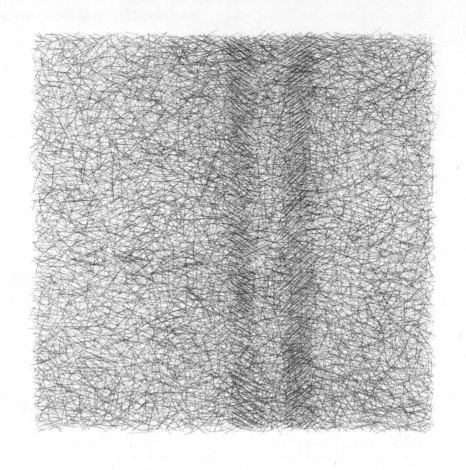

X.

As it neared midnight, she approached the entrance to the underworld.

It did not shimmer.

A door in the mountain opened, like a mouth, like an ear, like a cut.

She paused, she pulled out a handful of rough salt from a cloth pouch tied to her waist.

Rubbing the white rocks between her palms, she crushed them against each other and ground them down into smaller and smaller grains.

White crystals, translucent, but they captured the light from the moon and wouldn't let it go.

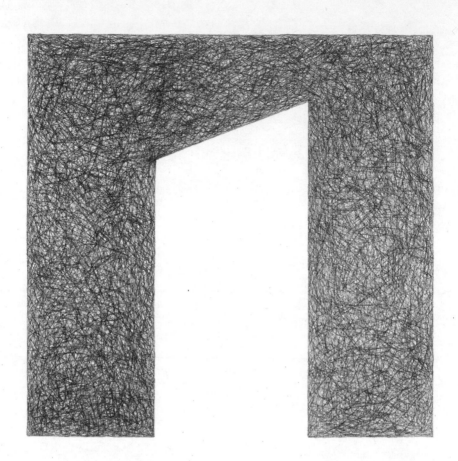

XI.

Another set of stairs, an escalator shimmered, then disappeared.

Baridegi stepped onto a circle of blackness.

And fell.

Down.

To the center of the world,

A shaft like a sentence.

All girls fall at the same rate.

She asked for the Water of Life from the King of the Underworld.

He said, *If . . .*

Tasks were given to her, for nine years, and Baridegi completed them all. Tasks for the unpassed spirits. These dead were immigrants, caught on the border between the world of the living and the underworld. She released them all, like a knife through a fruit stem.

She knit the air into white steam, a raft, a door, and opened it for the dead.

Then, red circles were painted on her cheeks and she married this King of the dead.

She bore him seven sons. One by one. A growing, breaking: squall, milk, eyes, skin, adore.

*

A jar of water appeared at her feet. She tied it to a wooden frame and put it on her back.

Her seven children followed her out of the mountain.

*

When she returned to her parents' palace, the gates opened for her. Her footfalls from years ago had turned the ground white.

Her father still, his body quiet on his raised bed, the four posters like flags.

Her mother, sisters regarded Baridegi with wonder.

Their silk dresses rustled as they leaned toward the bed.

Baridegi, the castaway, the returned, poured a drop of the water into his mouth.

And he awoke, and lived.

*

Out of her pouch tied to her waist, Baridegi brought forth a skein of red rope, the rope the king had dreamed about long before.

She handed one long red piece to her mother and each sister until there were none left.

Bowing low to her parents, she gazed downward, as if she could see through the doors of the earth.

She raised her children and put her ear to the doors of the sky.

For the rest of her long life, she dedicated herself to guiding spirits to the afterlife, helping the fallen, the wandering, and even the abandoned.

XII.

After many years, Baridegi's work was complete.

The King of the Underworld brought her a flask of the Water of Life.

It was surprisingly heavy, as if it were filled with dark silver.

As she walked out of his kingdom, she took out the small bag of salt and poured it out. The grains sank into the ground and disappeared.

(Section 4)

FATE IS A DEBT

The Wolvish Forage

The poetics of wolvish space and the displacement of air with the hot breath of the future.

I fell asleep in their den, which filled with night-serum, and the medicine became my lungs as I wandered through the rough carbon sleep of abandoned coal mines and saw my spirit panning for gold in the streams and creeks of the dead.

I saw us there.

Lingering over the remains of a spectacular
glittering feast.

Part I. Burn and Eat

Each day was a gorgeous wet machine with the rain-slicked bridge under the night bridge. We walked together along its swaying cables and let the water fall wanton from our necks.

I've written your undertow into my will, have signed it with a fistful of salt. This wound is my latest resort. My heart: its secret pangs like a muffled church bell. My eyes: hard gates.

You made me into a wolf. Before, I ate everything bleating and shivering. Before, I lay myself down.

You signed this contract. You summoned the wailing wall. You made a socket out of our last night.

We turned into swallows and sewed our open mouths, open to eat wind, open to make room for ghosts, open for the pack of wolves.

In this wolvish congress with the letters of the dead and my appetite for graffiti and my genuflection to the twenty-six occult symbols: leopards and glass and fury and waxwing flight.

Each day is a prince on his lesser throne with his lesser hate. His brother strange and left in the forest.

Every night is a widow.

What the outside woman craves is the strange testimony of the despot. The law and the police report in illegible half tongues.

If you could swallow scissors and thread and birth something durable. Birth your own face and body, but burning on the outside instead of the inside.

The despot is the gloat of caw and mercury and an army of centaurs en route to the farthest necropolis.

The pack of wolves inside me spent a year in silence. I studied the corpses of flight. I studied the architecture of wind, the ships breech birthed on surprised shores, coasts with chronic insomnia, facing always the wet suffocation of the great black fish with no face. The wolf pack gnaws on a manuscript of organs, each with a hood, each harboring its own verses.

Summon the heart's four-chambered congregation. We will chase our wolves through the starving blue to the piquant red. What kind of recovery does the tongue make in its dark, narrow room.

All the strange velvet inside me, rooms and rooms of it: a suite of crimes and a sibling, sharing duration, sharing a soldier's reprieve.

My body is a kind of necropolitan cradle, a museum blazing on the inside of the world's last night circus.

If I vanish after a certain conjuring, follow the spelling, follow the leopards with human hearts in their mouths, follow the scent of singed fur, as walking through flames is often required to renew the hollows of the world.

When I gave the wolves my opera glasses, binoculars, magnifying glass, telescope, pinhole camera, and a set of sharpened knives, they set fires all along the tree line.

They set to polishing the world's remaining lonely library carrels, eating the empty space along the way.

The perimeter of the bed is guarded by my soldier-wolves. The rough black of their scarves caught in my hair, binding my hands.

Part II. In the City of God

Perhaps born in a crime scene. Perhaps drawn from my mother as though an exorcism of pins and needles. Perhaps a child is a prosthesis and a pantomime. Perhaps a child is a cauterization of an oblivion.

No matter because I am a maker of tourniquets and a hawker of all the holy orders of the world.

God has chosen me. I leave the knitting of my white cloths and send the wolves inside me to the grotto with that vintage water from snowmelt. That water that tastes of the birth of planets, of the iron moon and its magnetic dreams writing roses all over the night.

We wear our skin like a priest disgraced in his winter hunger.

Perhaps my private hospital business will expand into purgatorial burial ritual and the eros of prayer. They will come from far and wide not to be stitched back together like dolls but to pay homage to me as if I were a man who hoards the calamitous light under his robes, a scholar of usury. Perhaps I was born to be a minister of handbills and rainwater.

A human-headed bird made its arrival night after night. I fell down upon things that are hidden during the day, which advance upon me at night, which draw my lightless body downward toward their receding forms, which remind me I have submerged the boat of my enemies and brought myself to silence.

I surrendered my mask and maps and deck of cards to God who made me his property without quarantine or inventory. A plate of ozone slipped under the cell door, the key made of mushrooms and eaten every morning. A shadow brings me a kind of a spike to bleed the humors. He promises new veins. He promises gifts like morphine and exams I've already taken.

In this city of God, all the stones rose surprised before me. The stigma of childhood marks my palms and feet. Orphaned by pain, I felt nothing, though I attempted repair of the body's summers through a kind of Christmas pageant.

Then, a swim through the dream of olive groves.

Then, the quilting of music into twelve gowns.
Then, the eating of worms.
Then, the gathering of incomplete births.
We fell upon the placenta still pulsing like a heart, and gorged on it like a pack of dogs.

We shall be purified. We were promised.
We were soaked in rum and honey and as drunk as choirboys.
Many anonymous eyes all over their unnamable bodies and their backs made blank for punishment.

One day, I was offered an advance cremation.
Why wait, I thought, let the gross body fall away, let me save the organs for later, let me fill these jars I have inherited from my mother's mother, let me empty them in that field down there.

Let me bury my brothers who come endlessly from over that hill, who come like a line of ants, like a swarm of bees, like a ring of fire.

Part III. Here I Will Abandon Laziness

From the eastern gate to the western gate, I made a womb out of a sparrow's nest, made every meal out of moss and the scorned end of each hour. I used my palm as a cutting board, made a child out of forbidden grammar. A grimoire, a child of pure glamour, a child not to be looked at directly, a child to walk ahead and not look back.

I orphaned myself every morning and every night.

I let the wolves out of my mouth at noon and swallowed them for dinner. I never fell into despair. I reused every letter, as frugal women are taught to do.

I wrote several martial epics while my husbands were away at the wars. I abandoned all ghosts who entered me with good intentions.

Unnatural Selection

The word *lottery* may come from the Latin *lot,*
meaning *fate,* or *destiny*.

and there we came upon / a child lottery / one stutter of brides /
waterwatereverywhere

religious feeling / a cape within / monk underground /
chthonic low-rise /

descend / count us all / my number / the registry /

game of chance / *a first draw* /

a desperate gamble /

here, king /

I /

I /

king, here /

gamble a desperate /

draw first / a chance of game /

register the number / my all / us count descend /

low-rise chronic underground / monk within cape / a feeling /

religious everywhere water / water brides / stutter /
one lottery / child upon / came we

there / and

A Black Box Theory of Descent

for the love of boxes

house	valley	a horse-mouth
goods	grave	the tongue makes a poor shovel
book	a back	a scalp a ragged flag
door	throne	bomb

boxes with open ends

a womb	its red	literacies
the eye	a white	camera
a tunnel	lonely	of light
the mouth	crime	and punishment

boxes with inner boxes

the grievous stomachs of cattle *(methanatos)*
marbled hearts of the dead
the woodland cottage and its oven and its beds and its ashy
dark hearth
a carton of matches and their quiet, time-release future fires

waiting boxes

a lady's dress hung over a chair
the oldest mirror in your house
your priest haunts the confessional
the placenta buried in the yard

for every child a ticket	or a stone
a barren woman	two stones
an old woman	three stones
a dead bee	a wax casket
a virgin	a white sail

deer, shot
man, shot

dinner
suicide

every ticket
no one fits inside

into the black box
but you fit inside

The Binding

inside the black box is the glory of God

is the glory of God an
untiring machine

the black input channels
stones of gold
led up the mountain

output channels of gold
to be stoned
first Isaac turned white from
foot to head

then Isaac's feet turned
next soft wool grew all over
he didn't notice
how animal skin is a herald
how he was becoming

cloven
his body
הָעֲקֵדָה (the binding)
of abandonment and woe
a black box

the inputs of God
the output of a son
a bleating sound
he stumbled

the father
he choked out
hoof to mouth in terror
onto the altar

Abraham bent above

as another black box
descended

Abraham's mouth open
an angel
a ram
child, a machine

the heavens entire
a nearby bush
blood
of trust and debt

Wheels of Misfortune

the best black box is a kind of wheel, like a foundling wheel / when that dark thing hardens from shadow to child

when you are that dark thing / when your mother is a wheel / you learn to haunt / hunt

when you open your mouth / great salt nets set us afloat / whale-road, the silver schools of fish, a thousand wheels of light /

a hero in the black box, torn and tattered / a boat unmade and remade / time shearing away from its raggedy corners / a finger prick, a splinter /

the black box of my holy burnt bones / what fires inside turn me to coal / my fine carbon mind / when dust or diamonds enter your brother's eye /

when the white witch gives birth to unnatural winter / at night, a chain mail of darkness descends over your eyes /

you count your organs for market / you weigh each one on golden scales / perfume and oil and coins for your eyes / each eye a wheel turned inward as if to sleep /

when children fall out of every rotation / like veils from the hanged woman / hanged by the weight of her own body / the force of gravity and desire / the eros of self-sufficiency /

the eros of the garment that carries one from life into death / the eros of all the mouths inside our bodies / one black box opening into another

In the House of Moths

Everything was white. My footprints—wet, then white. My shadow—
west, then white.

The dark concentric circles of my eyes—painted want, then white.
A house made of moths is light, weighing almost nothing, the walls
a thousand-thousand eyes, white on white. Glimmer. The murmur
of wander.

There was a grain to the air, a direction like fur, like sand. Sinkholes
appeared in all dimensions. The floor was alive.

I may have been dying. My desire for everything rose and fell and
flowered over and over.

My heart, a fathom of black seeds, rich with dark oil. Sound a fountain
recycling time arcing over the house of moths.

The electromagnetic field of mirrors made of honey-glass. An ear to
the floor and I was taken by the bees, their wings dipped in silver.

We walked, we walked through room after room as the house followed
me with its wings. What a handsome contagion.

Then, a clockface was a white door we were denied. I fashioned new
organs out of clouds as my body disassembled into water.

Dirt and grit and dust shook free from my open cloud-mouth. Many
white tools in my apron, I bent down to perform the critical mechanics
of Lepidoptera. We were jaws, we were many.

Wind, we were nothing.

Our Country Laundered Us

right into the paper, the forest, the breadcrumbs, the pebbles, the
stepmother, the father, the dead ~ mother, the broom, the cage,
the sugar, the flies, the tongue, the branch, ~ woman, the lingering
(laundering), ~ the bars and the branch, the zebra, the camel, the
sheep, ~ and the manger, the god and his angel, the devil, the birth, ~
the accident, the white light, the heat, ~ a curse, the burning, the
midnight ~ sacrifice, flight, finally, clean

(Section 5)

A WHITE FORKED FLAME

Sublime: Sailing Through a Midnight Sea

[utopias of descent, meditations on the sublime, the whale, the whiteness of insomnia, Wera Knoop, the insane husband and the selfsame drowned husband, the missing, the obsolete—]

fade in from black

Sublime

or

miel

that is to say

honey

a still shattered

of bees

a sub-nest

the anterior

interior

underneath

the hive

inside the hive

the queen

inside the queen

substitute

the young

heat of sound

limb

under sun

from the moon

asunder

assemble

resemble

emblem

tremble

tumble

tender

limn

and

enter

ETYMOLOGY

From Middle French *sublime*, from Latin *sublīmis* ("high"),
from *sub-* ("up to," "upward") + a root of uncertain affiliation,
often identified with Latin *līmis*, ablative singular of *līmus*
("oblique") or *līmen* ("threshold," "entrance," "lintel").

CHEMISTRY

verb (of a solid substance) change directly into vapor when
heated, typically forming a solid deposit again on cooling.

ARCHAIC

verb elevate to a high degree of moral or spiritual purity or excellence.

ANAGRAM

blueism

BLUEISM

noun (uncountable) (obsolete, derogatory) the possession or affectation of <u>learning</u> in a <u>woman</u>.

BLUESTOCKING

noun (derogatory) an intellectual or literary woman.

Elimbus

or

eliminate

this

business

to

nowhere

Erewhon

tropic of

utopia

Sir Thomas More

no place

geographies of face

the pleasures of

the body

they divide

into two

parts

all the space

within the belly

of the land

what with

rocks be very jeopardous

and dangerous

with people

that be no less

savage

fade out to white

Whiteness: A Spell Thrown

> "What the White Whale was to Ahab, has been hinted;
> what, at times, he was to me, as yet remains unsaid."

> —Chapter XLII, "The Whiteness of the Whale,"
> *Moby-Dick*

Though in many natural objects, **whiteness refiningly enhances beauty**, as if imparting some special virtue of its own, as in marbles, japonicas, and pearls; and though various nations have in some way recognised a certain royal pre-eminence in this hue; **even** the **barbaric**, grand old kings of Pegu placing the title "Lord of the White Elephants" above all their other magniloquent ascriptions of dominion; and the modern kings of **Siam** unfurling the same snow-white quadruped in the royal standard; and the Hanoverian flag bearing the **one figure of a snow-white** charger; and the great **Austrian Empire,** Caesarian, heir to overlording Rome, having for the imperial color the same imperial hue; and though this pre-eminence in it applies to the **human race itself**, giving the **white man** ideal **mastership over every dusky tribe**; and though, besides all this, **whiteness has been** even made significant of **gladness**, for among the Romans **a white** stone marked a joyful **day**; and though in other mortal sympathies and symbolizings, this same hue is made the emblem of many touching, noble things - the **innocence of brides**, the benignity of age; though among the Red Men of America the giving of the white belt of wampum was the deepest pledge of honor; though in many climes, **whiteness** typifies the **majesty of Justice** in the ermine of the Judge, and contributes to the daily state of **kings and queens** drawn by **milk-white steeds**; though even in the higher mysteries of the most august religions it has been made the **symbol of** the **divine spotlessness and power**; by the Persian fire worshippers, the **white forked flame** being held the **holiest on** the **altar**; and in the Greek mythologies, **Great Jove himself** made incarnate in a **snow-white bull**; and though to the noble Iroquois, the midwinter sacrifice of the sacred White Dog was by far the holiest festival of their theology, that spotless, faithful creature being held the purest envoy they could send to the Great Spirit with the annual tidings of their own fidelity; and though directly from the **Latin word for white**, all Christian priests derive the name of one part of their **sacred vesture**, the alb or tunic, worn beneath the cassock; and though among the holy pomps of the Romish faith, **white is** specially employed in the celebration of **the Passion of our Lord**; though in the Vision of St. John, **white robes** are given to the **redeemed**, and the four- and-twenty elders stand clothed in white before the **great white throne**, and the **Holy One** that sitteth there **white like wool**; yet for all these accumulated associations, with whatever is **sweet**, and **honorable**, and **sublime**, there yet lurks an elusive something in the **innermost idea** of this hue, which **strikes more** of **panic to the soul** than that redness which affrights in blood.

This elusive quality it is, which causes the **thought of whiteness**, when divorced from more kindly associations, and **coupled with any object terrible** in itself, to **heighten** that **terror** to the **furthest bounds**. Witness the **white bear of the poles**, and the **white shark of the tropics**; what but their **smooth, flaky whiteness** makes them the **transcendent horrors** they are? That **ghastly whiteness** which imparts such an **abhorrent mildness,** even more **loathsome** than terrific, to the **dumb gloating** of their aspect. So that not the fierce-fanged tiger in his heraldic coat can so stagger courage as the **white-shrouded** bear or shark.

Bethink thee of the **albatross**, whence come those clouds of spiritual wonderment and **pale dread**, in which that **white phantom** sails in all imaginations? Not Coleridge **first threw that spell**; but God's great, unflattering laureate, Nature . . .

Fish Scales All Over This Ark

dear God why did you call me to make jealous heirs / give me a wife
and more wives / break all these trees to matches / leave me the moon's
remorse /

for you for them the dandelions and the albatross / for you for them
the prow to cripple sheets of ice / for you for them the deep breath and
the dive into the whale's mouth / for you for them grasp the baleen and
glide past the vast bellows the lungs the heart /

for me for me the oil lamp fires at night lighting the deck of the ship /
for me for me a hundred *hundred* birthdays and a mantle of shark skins /
for me for me sail the world in search of ivory daggers /

for them for them the bottom of the ocean / for them for them the
night-stallions of sirens and the king of corals / for them for them the
end of the world the steam rising from the houses of worship /

for them for them not the love of god but *gesture wave motion perpetual
motion*

Ravishing Migrations

Invisible hands build a fleet of ships to rival the Japanese, the Persians, the British Navy / Sightless eyes fashion cannons and point them unerringly toward the enemy /

The enemy in watery stereo sound like dolphins like whales like the names of generals / The enemy in the black sky and below the blue ground /

Secret tunnels warrens of the young the chain of command the tanks and the bombs / Walk over this earth so smooth of basalt / Walk through this wall for treasure pull your ancestors through the eye of a needle /

Strap the child to your back and your shaman's rattle the last cry / Leave the child that is no longer your child but the ground's child / Like a stone bury the body / Watch how a stone drinks rain as if parched / Watch how a stone grows moss like hair /

Make a cairn of children and listen to their gossip / Watch them pretend to be alive / Look into their pitted eyes and close them with a song /

Leave the song there and move your feet over the land / Break it down and leave it everywhere / Until you have nothing /

Until you leave your name behind because it is so heavy and you are so very light

Transit from Lintel to Lintel

travelers, wipe the blood off your shoes / lay low with lambs /

a blue accordion of white weather / whether bird night nor black-eyed morning /

hoop of horizon beneath, a sum, a transit / angle of repose / old marine permanently under dusk / sky a gold-hoard, light-road /

nerves customize the nightfall garden / nocturnal collegium of snakes / your sovereign branding /

your reveries with a gilded hoof / you kick like a mule / clandestine bit and bridle /

drowned tongue and underground tide / slant rhyming chants of the children, building, hiding, sorting, sparing /

command: approach, ride and rider—

My First Voyage Out

Why upon your first voyage as a passenger, did you yourself
feel such a mystical vibration, when first told that you
and your ship were now out of sight of land?

—*Moby-Dick*

{Figure in murky light} {Didn't you know time travel leaves invisible
brands on the skin?} {Back then, we practiced with black light we
plagiarized from the future} {We time the known variables of the arrival
stages} {"Godspeed, tomorrow."} {You found abundant time to design
the machine.} {Everything made the rain black and scaled} {Well,
misfortune, you perch in the sky, fevering the ground} {Under no purse,
no past, no paterfamilias} {We made death masks with all the gold}

{Contort the dead comfortable with suffocation} {The dead anathema
to air} {Always are the dead getting to spend the old currency} {They
knew that everything burns at a singular rate} {Fortified the deck of
cards, deck of stockades} {But time has an extravagant spinal span
like the world's snake} {Sky dives through the axis wrenches the
tactics} {All the cousins' plans hard to read, ride taut and dark} {Never
untethered forefather and foreshadow} {Halo overhead, an electric
meadow of florets} {Paragraphs of bees a suspense of burn} {Painted
sail stays a spell}

{Never powered my machine my platinum container of holes} {Always
the holes are my titanium mother and her tin mother, too} {Scratch my
hand like my hands are the rippling backs of cats} {My hands fit the
metal into slighter and lesser boxes} {As a woman I can fold anything}
{I corrugate time into layers of a cake, a cloak} {Can't you all pleat and
tuck a cart, a cast} {For when I sew myself into the pilot seat} {The
passenger seat is sometimes there, sometimes not} {Once there were a
hundred passenger seats} {All around, all around} {Asunder, things are
always growing when I'm not looking} {When I'm not looking things
are always going around my back}

{Hospital to ride alongside me} {Burned parade trailings to ride along inside me} {Fluttering petals' flags taking me into their confidence} {Neon yellow every brand of sunshine to turn one side of me aside} {We hiked together, procured the last book they offered at the library} {Tourism had tumbled out of vogue}

{We shed our compulsions like dead microbiota} {They fell through us like pages of dead skin} {Wonder-worn, I put the sheets through my typewriter} {Masked all things in the past made of fur} {Every child needed to be combed and untangled} {Black teeth I went through ribbon after ribbon} {The length of each stretch I plaited into everything} {Gothic immoderate hairpiece, braided dress, new spools of time} {Dusky and inky like a shot glass of hot octopus panic} {Baroque November already in my cathedral of conceivable futures} {Central nervous system I think I'll go back to May}

{Unearthed my childhood safety scissors with the rubber-dipped handles and robbed the deck of cards and fashioned myself a new mother} {Ghost reappropriated all the angles} {Stacked and plunged them in the thick air of an open boat} {Time pelts me, a creature} {Phantasm dressed myself in sailcloth} {Hallucinated the sea} {Kindled with salt-stiff hair} {Had wedded a mermaid} {Left her seaweed coronet on my open throat} {Whalebone trident ice pick, my dagger, my arrow} {I transcribed all the instructions for myself in the moss} {We chewed the rule books and swallowed hard} {Engraving itself inside me on the way down} {Coffin warehouses} {Pure descent with a moss baby in every coffin} {In every mouth a moss baby dwindling through the stars of the esophagus} {Our favored snake begins at the nether of my throat} {I appointed that new star Peristalta}

{Oak cask new year of my childhood my father made a coffin to fit around me} {The eve of my birthday the slighter coffin dismantled} {I always feel the world blink bright} {I use a gold stopwatch} {This mountain has moved the hands of the clock back and forth like a cradle} {My face rusts while I languish in the past} {We flag in the past with the rearguard, with the older horses} {I sewed my bridle from the skin of my cousin} {We bridle, bride, board, bird} {We flee and fly}

{Forward I sling a rifle like a beauty queen's ribbon} {Multiply I collect terse salutes from the jubilant crowd} {Fertile like the collection box at church} {Unwatered family names carefully tendered and ledgered} {Sky-white envelopes open like mouths} {The lank twenty-dollar bill like an old tongue} {Ash that makes no sense when I bring it to the past} {I can see you black and blue} {Uncount a thousand babies floating on lotus flowers} {the color of abandon} {open mouths, swallowing the dark} {Serious pious each of them stitching the space suits}

{Can you hand-press a baby out of brine} {What do we see after we escape the machine} {Soot on the knees of our space suit} {Fortune favors silver crowns of armored fish} {My mermaid wife turning to iron} {Bubbles escape from the flanks of my mask} {Records of the world above, sinkers fashioned to appear as white moths} {Renamed for constellations, renamed for the arrow}

Tiger | *Fade In, Fade Out*

"Tragically, the death of Korea's last wild tiger foreshadowed the end of Korea's unity. During the tumult of the Japanese occupation, just before the nation was torn in two at the end of the Korean War, the last Korean tiger faded quietly into folklore."

The tiger began its solo evolution, splitting from what would become the snow leopard 3.2 million years ago.

Queens of the night.

Scientists call this the Pliocene Epoch.

Fact one: tigers are less closely related to lions, leopards, and jaguars than those cats are to each other.

Fact two: The blue whale, the bumblebee bat, and you and I are placental mammals.

Fact three:

"All of these creatures, in their wondrous array of shapes and sizes, evolved from small, unassuming, scurrying insect-eaters that lived a few hundred thousand years after the apocalypse that finished off most of the dinosaurs.

A team of U.S. scientists have now reconstructed what this ancestral placental was like, to an extraordinary level of detail. They have predicted how much it would have weighed, the number of molars in its jaws, the shape of its sperm, and the path that its carotid artery took up its neck. None of this comes from a fossil of the creature itself. Instead, the predictions are based on 80 of its descendants, including some that are still alive and others that joined it in extinction."

It resembles a mouse, with a longer more primitive-
looking face, and longer, sharper teeth.

Mother. Grandmother. Granduncle. Cousin.

Littermate. Ancestral placental mammal.

Each of us had our own personal ocean.

It spilled as we played the lethal game of edibility, impermanence,
curse, and cease.

Like a cross between a labyrinth and a night flower, we bloomed.

Died and gave way. Died and gave way.

Wave after wave.

*

Before the last tiger departed these pine forests
for the pristine underworld, he was a man,
he was a god. It hurts me to write this.
It hurts me to acknowledge male creatures as gods,
as lords of the sky and the field.

In each soldier I see an animal's heart,
more purple than red, flush with fear—

Blood ready to leap like a fish through the rivers of the body.
Young body, the brand-new body of this world.

Where paradise turns to brush fires, to corpses.

Teach me to cut grass, to twist strands like hair into rope.
A homemade casket.

Teach me how to die away from this green world.

We taught you how to live, how to blend into the evening forest floor;
how the will to survive is a mantle to wear and discard.

We did live among each other like brother and sister,
dream and enemy. My white teeth.

Steam rises from my coat. Swallow the sun.

Evolution in the Underworld

Vocabulary lessons in the afterlife become affairs of high ritual. To hold a wood pencil in the hand again is a great pleasure. A hexagon to keep it from rolling away, to provide rest and silence, readiness. The dark sheen of the graphite letters appearing on the white paper. We make a kind of drunkenness of it. A line never was so handsome.

Touching the paper as if it might be skin. With more I could draw and fill in a shadow for each of us. To make our own marks again as we did up above. I have nearly forgotten how bright it could be—as if the sun fell open like a cut lemon.

Time fluttered away like old paper. Burials of things were a form of magic. To cast a spell, to find the right person among all the persons of the underworld. To wait for the right person to arrive below, as if lowered on a thread. To practice patience like a spider in the dark. To be held by an invisible web, to feel gravity gently pull on your limbs like a lover.

To sit like a monk, with bombs raining all above—this is the one roof that will hold against. Why must the living assault us with their language? Crematorium, mausoleum, interment, as if Latin were still alive on paper to make containers for the dead. We have our own coliseum. We have a circus. We remember bread and distractions.

Each week we sit down to our lessons like cats waiting for a mouse parade. Hungry for words, for soft strings of them. As if we had brought an army of silk worms with us, to serve us. We recall our first word: *panoply. a complete or impressive collection of things. a splendid display. a complete set of arms or suit of armor.* The death of completion. A kind of printmaking. Engraving. An impression, some kind of print on something yielding.

Desire moves through glass to the objects on the other side. This perpetual motion is a liquid like gold. Try to remember the difference between solid and vapor. What is heat. The excitement of molecules and rearrangement of the spirit. Electricity follows me, still, a personal weather. My school mimics the cosmos.

Our school welcomes the dead with a mantle of petals. We have a panoply of orchards. We have everything of everything. Everything you lost is here. You are what others have lost.

You are here. Finally, there is enough.

The others, the others who lost you? They will find you here, in the school, in the school of infinity.

Lullaby | *Goodnight*

A song for seventh children

Goodnight, parents' first chance encounter.
Goodnight, ovum, alone.
Goodnight, placenta.
Goodnight, fetal dreams.

*

Goodnight, hearing the Korean language through water, blood,
and mother-skin.
Goodnight, birthing process, crowning, crown.
Goodnight, baby, *exit wound*, you.
Goodnight, (Korean) name.
Goodnight, family registry and list of fathers and fathers and fathers
and further, farther.

*

Goodnight, sister(s).
Goodnight, brother(s).
Goodnight, 엄마 umma and 아빠 appa.
Goodnight, 할머니 halmoni and 외할머니 oehalmoni
Goodnight, 할아버지 haraboji and 외할아버지 oeharaboji

*

Goodnight, singular moon over the roof of our dwelling.
Goodnight, mother's milk.
Goodnight, scent of mother's neck.
Goodnight, _____ .
Goodnight, foster family–five adults and a dog.
Goodnight, homeland.
Goodnight, fellow citizens.

Goodnight, ancestral tongue.
Goodnight, memory and its imprints.

*

Goodnight, Park Chung-hee and assassins.
Goodnight, Park's wife Yuk Young-soo, and high school student,
    Jang Bong-hwa.
Goodnight, Smith and Wesson 36.
Goodnight, Park Geun-hye, Korea's first woman president, daughter
    of Park Chung-hee.
Goodnight, impeachment.

*

Goodnight, reunification.
Goodnight, going to bed with one face.
Goodnight, waking up in another country.
Goodnight, waking up in a-------- house.
Goodnight, waking up in a-------- family.
Goodnight, waking up in a-------- name.
Goodnight, wetlands of the body.
Goodnight, fever dreams and fugue states.
Goodnight, tomb guardians.
Goodnight, graves of my ancestors.
Goodnight, soju poured on headstones.

*

Goodnight, merging into the crowd.
Goodnight, family medical history (Throat cancer? Heart attacks?
    Madness? Suicide? Patricide? . . .).
Goodnight, grandparents of my (American) (Korean) children.
Goodnight, Other Self and your Other Life.
Goodnight, everything.

*

                                   I will take my body to America.
                        She remembers (everything) in her own way.
                                                She attends me.

*

(Princess, of a kingdom of one.)
In a sense, I kidnapped her.
She (always) has to go
Where (ever)
I (may) (I) go—

APPENDIX

L'Etranger | *An Unburial* | *A Funeral*

Korean words for family

> "After you died I could not hold a funeral,
> and so my life became a funeral."
>
> —Han Kang, *The Vegetarian*

> "The feeling that she had never really lived in this world caught her by
> surprise. It was a fact. She had never lived. Even as a child, as far back
> as she could remember, she had done nothing but endure."
>
> —Han Kang, *The Vegetarian*

This is true: My daughter had the words for mother and daughter
tattooed on her fingers last year.

I realized I did not know the Korean word for *daughter.* 딸.
Pronounced: ttal.

I had to resort to a concise Wikipedia entry to see all the words for
Korean family relationships. Throughout my life I am imagining,
constructing, dissolving, and missing these relationships that for me
don't even exist on paper. A deconstructed and generic family tree like
the one in this entry is strangely satisfying as an archetype and map of
what could have been.

Family and kinship terms in Korean:

- grandparents: 조부모
  - grandfather: 할아버지
  - grandmother: 할머니
  - maternal grandfather: 외할아버지
  - maternal grandmother: 외할머니

- parents: 부모
  - father: 아버지
  - mother: 어머니

- spouse: 배우자
  - husband: 남편
  - wife: 아내

- in-laws:
  - parents-in-law: 처부모 (wife's parents), 시부모 (husband's parents)
    - father-in-law: 장인 (wife's father), 시아버지 (husband's father)
    - mother-in-law: 장모 (wife's mother), 시어머니 (husband's mother)
  - son-in-law: 사위
  - daughter-in-law: 며느리
  - brother-in-law: 처남 (wife's brother), 자형 (older sister's husband) 매부 (younger sister's husband), 시숙 (husband's brother)
    - wife's younger brother: 처남
  - sister-in-law: 형수 (older brother's wife), 제수/계수 (younger brother's wife)
    - wife's older sister: 처형
    - wife's younger sister: 처제

- son: 아들
- daughter: 딸
- siblings: 형제자매; 형제
  - brother
    - elder brother: 형 (male's brother), 오빠 (female's brother)
    - younger brother: 동생, 남동생
  - sister(s): 누이; 자매
    - elder sister: 누나 (of a male), 언니 (of a female)
    - younger sister: 동생, 여동생, 누이동생

- uncle: 아저씨 (only for more distant uncles)
  - paternal uncle: 삼촌 (father's unmarried younger brother), 큰아버지 (father's older brother, irrespective of marital

status), 작은아버지 (father's married younger brother), 고모부 (고모's husband)

- ○ maternal uncle: 외삼촌 (mother's brother, regardless of relative age or marital status), 이모부 (이모's husband)

- aunt: 숙모 (parent's brother's wife), 큰어머니 (큰아버지's wife), 작은어머니 (작은아버지's wife), 고모 (father's sister), 이모 (mother's sister), 아줌마 (more distant relations)
- cousin: 사촌; 남자사촌 (*m*); 여자사촌 (*f*)
- nephew/niece: 조카
- niece: 조카딸, 질녀
- grandchild
  - ○ grandson: 손자, 외손자 (daughter's son)
  - ○ granddaughter: 손녀, 외손녀 (daughter's daughter)

SOURCES

Epigraph by Craig Santos Perez, from "Halloween in the Anthropocene, 2015," Poetry Foundation (website), accessed October 15, 2021. https://www.poetryfoundation.org/poetrymagazine/poems/88745/halloween-in-the-anthropocene-2015.

Definition of "Hag" paraphrased from *Online Etymology Dictionary* (website), accessed October 6, 2021. https://www.etymonline.com/word/hag?ref=etymonline_crossreference.

Numbers 5:23, Holy Bible, King James Version, sourced from Knowing Jesus (website), accessed October 6, 2021. https://bible.knowing-jesus.com/Numbers/5/23.

In "Castaways in Paradise," the personal passport is from the Ministry of Foreign Affairs, Republic of Korea, issued April 16, 1975, and is courtesy of the author. The text on the left is from book 2 of "Of Mortal Children," in Ovid's *Metamorphoses,* translated by Charles Martin. The text on the right is from *Columbus: The Four Voyages 1492–1504* by Laurence Bergreen.

"Women in Korean myths . . ." a quote from 김혜순 Kim Hyesoon, from "Kim Hyesoon: The Female Grotesque," by Ruth Williams in *Guernica. Guernica Magazine* (website), accessed October 14, 2021. https://www.guernicamag.com/williams_kim_1_1_12.

"Tiger" info from "Korean Tigers Back from the Brink of Extinction, but Not in South Korea," Expertsure.com (website), accessed October 15, 2021. https://www.expertsure.com/2008/11/24/korean-tigers-back-from-the-brink-of-extinction-but-not-in-south-korea.

ACKNOWLEDGMENTS

Thank you to my ancestors, without whom I would not exist.

Thank you to the land and water, without whom this paper (and everything) would not exist.

This book was written mostly within the boundaries of the city of Minneapolis, in the U.S. state of Minnesota, which is on the homelands of the Dakota people. As an immigrant to the U.S., I am a settler, occupier, and uninvited guest. Decolonization is not possible without giving back land (Eve Tuck and K. Wayne Yang).

A poetry book is the result of collective labor across space and time. Thank you to everyone at and involved with Coffee House Press: especially wonderful and generous editor Erika Stevens; Anitra Budd; Carla Valadez; Daley Farr; Lizzie Davis; Rob Keefe, whom I've known and worked with for years; Marit Swanson; Zoë Koenig; Quynh Van; Enrique Olivarez; fall 2021 interns, Adrianna Jereb and Anita Stasson; and series editors, Valeria Luiselli, Youmna Chlala, and Ken Chen. Thank you to the board of directors and funders and donors. Thank you all for making beautiful books that play a part in keeping American and world literature surprising, relevant, and serious.

Thank you to designer Christina Vang for working with us to create this gorgeous and mysterious cover.

Enduring appreciation for the late Allan Kornblum, founder of the press in 1972, and also for Chris Fischbach, former editor and publisher, who said *yes* to my first poetry manuscript, and to my second, third, and this, my fourth. Having a publishing home at Coffee House Press for my poetry since 2006 has been the backbone of my life as a writer, and its importance to me and my path as a poet cannot be overstated.

Special thanks to Canadian collaborators Godfre Leung, curator of the Unstately exhibit, a yearlong series of programs on fiction and the nation-state; Bopha Chhay, director of ArtSpeak in Vancouver; graphic designer Victoria Lum; and illustrator and collaborator Jinny

Yu, without whom the book's long sequence about the first Korean shaman, and the entire chapbook *granted to a foreign citizen*, could not have been created, exhibited, or published. Working with an entire Asian North American creative team was so safe, creative, and inspiring, and is a gift that keeps on giving.

Thank you very much to independent publicist and writer of exquisite poems Jennifer Huang for your skillful, knowledgeable, and persistent work to give my books their best chance at connecting with readers. Please read Huang's debut poetry collection, *Return Flight*, winner of the 2021 Ballard Spahr Prize for Poetry and published in January 2022 by Milkweed Editions. This book "is a lush reckoning: with inheritance, with body, with trauma, with desire—and with the many tendons in between."

Special thanks to my beloved Minneapolis poetry community: Ánh-Hoa Thị Nguyễn, Su Hwang, Merle Geode, Rachel Moritz, Sean Garrison Phillips, Taiyon Coleman, Valérie Déus, Heid E. Erdrich, Michael Kleber-Diggs, David Lawrence Grant, Michael Torres, Roy Guzmán, Lisa Marie Brimmer, Junauda Petrus-Nasah, Chris Martin, Mary Austin Speaker, Matt Rasmussen, D. Allen, Chaun Webster, Hye-Kyong Kim, IBé, Andrea Jenkins, Rodrigo Sanchez-Chavarria, Venessa Fuentes, Sherry Quan Lee, Bao Phi, Ed Bok Lee, David Mura, Ifrah Mansour, Ty Chapman, Jennifer Kwon Dobbs, Sagirah Shahid, Chris Santiago, Greg Hewett, Dobby Gibson, Michael Bazzett, Hieu Minh Nguyen, Albert Lee, Saymoukda Duangphouxay Vongsay, May Lee-Yang, Chavonn Williams Shen, Anthony Ceballos, Heidi Czerwiec, Sarah Fox, Paula Cisewski, Moheb Soliman, Rosetta Peters, Marion Gómez, Matt Mauch, Hans Weyandt, Hawona Sullivan Janzen, Deborah Keenan, and many more! (Yes, some of you live in St. Paul.) And much appreciation and deep respect and admiration for Minnesota's poet laureate, and first Native poet to hold this role, the wonderful Gwen Westerman.

Enduring appreciation to everyone in the extraordinary Kundiman family and the Asian American Writers' Workshop community, for all you do and have done over the years for Asian American writers and Asian American literature/s. The diaspora(s) is/are boundless, protean, generative, visionary, and brilliant. The way you create and hold community is world-changing cultural work that will continue to impact this country and beyond in the years and decades to come. Thank you for making homes for us.

Thank you to fellow Korean American poets and writers for their support, inspiration, advocacy, community service, and literary citizenship and pathfinding, including Sarah Park Dahlen, Grace Cho, Arlene Kim, Jane Jeong Trenka, Lee Herrick, Matthew Salesses, Sueyeun Juliette Lee, Janice Lee, Christy Namee Eriksen, Kim Park Nelson, Eric Sharp, Naomi Ko, Yurie Hong, Kimberly McKee, Victoria Cho, Tiana Nobile, E. J. Koh, Leah Silvieus, Marci Calabretta Cancio-Bello, Margaret Rhee, Sarah Richards Graba, Myung Mi Kim, Nicole Chung, Mary-Kim Arnold, Arhm Choi Wild, Bo Schwabacher, Ishle Yi Park, Don Mee Choi, Minsoo Kang, Cathy Park Hong, Jae-Ha Kim, Nami Mun, and Min Jin Lee, and special thanks to Marie Myung-Ok Lee and Alexander Chee for founding and sustaining the Fourth Kingdom community (since 2011!) and being spectacular public intellectuals and artists.

Grateful for the writerly and artistic camaraderie, visions, and community-building of Carolyn Holbrook, Kathy Haddad, Kao Kalia Yang, Dameun Strange, Xiaolu Wang, Shen Xin, Diane Wilson, John Coy, Louise Erdrich, Marcie Rendon, Shannon Gibney, thomas carlson, Craig Farmer, Anne Dennison, Leah Larson, Sung Ja Shin, Wing Young Huie, V. V. Ganeshananthan, G. E. Patterson, Lina Jamoul, Kou B. Thao, Sharon Her, Gabrielle Civil, Purvi Shah, Maria Damon, Michelle Naka Pierce, Marco Wilkinson, Blake Edward Hamilton, Eileen Tabios, Anne Waldman, Kazim Ali, Craig Santos Perez, Sean Singer, Hoa Nguyen, Saara Myrene Raappana, Kathryn Kysar, Jen Bowen, Mike Alberti, Sam Gould, Marlon James, Mona Susan Power, Rupa Thadani, Julia Dinsmore, Cristeta Boarini, Samantha Sencer-Mura, Corinth Matera, Emmanuel Ortiz, Mélina Mangal, Bo Thao-Urabe, Kate Nuernberger, Tasslyn Magnuson, Sheila O'Connor, Anna Meyer, Roxanne Anderson, Mike Hoyt, Diver Van Avery, Miré Regulus, Zarlasht Niaz, Senah Yeboah-Sampong, Witt Siasoco, Chitra Vairavan, Susan Raffo, Sara Wernick Schonwald, Alejandra Tobar-Alatriz, Emily Perez, the late Meena Alexander, Abayomi Animashaun, Mark Nowak, and many more who directly or indirectly have helped me and many others live, think, and work as poets.

Thank you to all of the curators and venues that have hosted me in the past few years as I presented some of the work included in *The Wet Hex*. Many of these poems have been published in journals and anthologies; thank you to *POETRY*; the 2021 Gwangju Biennale; the Unstately exhibit; Solidarity Street Gallery, Second Shift Studio; Pollen Midwest; *The Portable Boog Reader II; Indiana Review; Women : Poetry : Migration, an anthology;* Mapping North exhibit, Form + Content Gallery; *Hyphen: Asian America Unabridged; DUSIE; We Are Meant to Rise: Voices for Justice from Minneapolis to the World;* and *South Minneapolis*.

Special thank you to the fellow teachers, writing students, partners, supporters, and program alumni of the Minnesota Prison Writing Workshop for reminding me of the value of language and its relationship to freedom. Thank you to PEN America. Thank you to poets Reginald Dwayne Betts, Natalie Diaz, and Dionne Brand for your support of incarcerated writers, and for your most recent poetry collections, which were a pleasure and provocation to read and teach.

I am grateful to the voters of Minnesota for supporting the arts; this manuscript was written with the support of two Minnesota State Arts Board grants. Big thank you to program officer and fellow writer Sherrie Fernandez-Williams, and everyone who works to support artists through these kinds of redistributive funding opportunities. Thank you also to the Foundation for Contemporary Arts for support in the form of an Emergency Grant, COVID-19 Bridge Fund.

I apologize sincerely to anyone I should have thanked who I have missed. I've been the recipient of a great deal of generosity and grace in my twenty-five years of working at poetry, and in the past six years since my last book of poems was published.

Thank you to my children Jae and Ty for being fun and funny and sweet and yourselves. Thank you to my brother D. and sister-in-law S. for being great, especially through these past years of parental loss. Thank you to D. B. for all your love, support, good humor, good cooking, patience, pandemic life-ing, and big dreams.

Coffee House Press began as a small letterpress operation in 1972 and has grown into an internationally renowned nonprofit publisher of literary fiction, essay, poetry, and other work that doesn't fit neatly into genre categories.

Coffee House is both a publisher and an arts organization. Through our *Books in Action* program and publications, we've become interdisciplinary collaborators and incubators for new work and audience experiences. Our vision for the future is one where a publisher is a catalyst and connector.

LITERATURE
is not the same thing as
PUBLISHING

FUNDER ACKNOWLEDGMENTS

Coffee House Press is an internationally renowned independent book publisher and arts nonprofit based in Minneapolis, MN; through its literary publications and *Books in Action* program, Coffee House acts as a catalyst and connector—between authors and readers, ideas and resources, creativity and community, inspiration and action.

Coffee House Press books are made possible through the generous support of grants and donations from corporations, state and federal grant programs, family foundations, and the many individuals who believe in the transformational power of literature. This activity is made possible by the voters of Minnesota through a Minnesota State Arts Board Operating Support grant, thanks to the legislative appropriation from the Arts and Cultural Heritage Fund. Coffee House also receives major operating support from the Amazon Literary Partnership, Jerome Foundation, McKnight Foundation, Target Foundation, and the National Endowment for the Arts (NEA). To find out more about how NEA grants impact individuals and communities, visit www.arts.gov.

Coffee House Press receives additional support from Bookmobile; Dorsey & Whitney LLP; Elmer L. & Eleanor J. Andersen Foundation; Fredrikson & Byron, P.A.; the Matching Grant Program Fund of the Minneapolis Foundation; Mr. Pancks' Fund in memory of Graham Kimpton; the Schwab Charitable Fund; and the U.S. Bank Foundation.

THE PUBLISHER'S CIRCLE OF COFFEE HOUSE PRESS

Sun Yung Shin is a Korean-born poet, writer, collaborative artist, and bodyworker. She/they lives in Minneapolis.

The Wet Hex was designed by Bookmobile Design & Digital Publisher Services. Text is set in PT Serif.